Clement
Temple
Blackfreyars
The Globe

Nicholas Rowe's *The Life of William Shakespeare*, published in 1709 as the preface to his pioneering edition of the plays, is the first biography of Shakespeare, and all subsequent research is indebted to it. It is also one of the earliest biographies of any writer in English. Working less than a century after Shakespeare's death, Rowe, helped by the great actor Thomas Betterton (who owned the 'Chandos' portrait of Shakespeare reproduced on the cover) was able to collect folk memories of Shakespeare in Stratford, as well as undertaking original archival research. The result is no dry academic exercise, however; Rowe was himself a poet and playwright, and his style is always energetic and engaging. As Charles Nicholl explains in his introduction, Rowe's essay is both a landmark in Shakespeare studies and a fascinating glimpse into the early 18th-century literary imagination.

This edition is illustrated with reproductions from the frontispieces to the plays in Rowe's edition: not only the first illustrations of Shakespeare, but a unique record of early Shakespearean performance.

THE LIFE OF

WILLIAM SHAKESPEARE

Martin Droeshout sculpsit London.

THE LIFE OF WILLIAM SHAKESPEARE

Nicholas Rowe

WITH AN INTRODUCTION BY
Charles Nicholl

PALLAS ATHENE

The Globe

CONTENTS

NICHOLAS ROWE Esq[re]

M. V[dr] Gucht Sculp.

INTRODUCTION

Charles Nicholl

WHAT NICHOLAS ROWE (1674–1718) CALLED *Some Account of the Life &c of Mr. William Shakespear* was written as a preface to his handsome new edition of the plays, published in six volumes in 1709. It is often described as the first biography of Shakespeare. There have been many hundreds of them since – longer, weightier, more probing and indeed more factually accurate – but three centuries after its appearance Rowe's brief biographical sketch still deserves to be taken seriously.

He was writing nearly a century after Shakespeare's death (1616), beyond the arc of living memory and firsthand testimony, and with little in the way of printed sources to draw on. Some vaguely biographical material could be gleaned from the introduction to the First Folio (1623), edited by Shakespeare's former colleagues, John Heminges and Henry Condell. Ben Jonson's

Opposite: Nicholas Rowe, engraving by Michael Vandergucht after a portrait by Sir Godfrey Kneller, 1715

Timber (1640), Thomas Fuller's *Worthies of England* (1662), John Dryden's *Essay of Dramatic Poesy* (1668) and Gerard Langbaine's *Account of the English Dramatick Poets* (1691) offered a few scattered comments and anecdotes. The researches of John Aubrey, an expert though not always reliable sniffer-out of information, had turned up some interesting details, but they remained in a chaotic bundle of unedited manuscripts, and there is no sign that Rowe had any knowledge of them.

These are the antecedents of Rowe's *Account* – disjointed bits of biographical information and tradition: '*tamquam tabula naufragi*' ('like the fragments of a shipwreck'), in Aubrey's vivid phrase. Rowe's is the first to attempt to put them together, to produce a fuller narrative 'account' rather than just individual items – indeed the word 'account' conveys this, its financial conotation suggesting suggest a metaphorical reckoning up of a man's life.

The appetite which Rowe sees himself as satisfying was to some extent a new one. How 'fond' people are, he says, 'for any little personal story of the great men of antiquity, their families, the common accidents of their lives, and even their shape, make and features... How trifling soever this curiosity may seem to be, it is certainly very natural.' Nowadays we take this curiosity for granted, but at the beginning of the eighteenth century the art of biography was still in its infancy. Its first heyday would come some decades later, with such works as Samuel Johnson's *Lives of the Poets* (1779-81) and James Boswell's great *Life of Johnson* (1791). It is from this later period, and from this literary circle, that we have the first full-length, scholarly biography of Shakespeare – Edmond Malone's, published in 1790.

ROWE'S BIOGRAPHY IS NO MATCH FOR MALONE'S, but it is an important finger-post towards it – important as a gathering of data and impressions into something resembling a portrait of the man, and important also because of the style and panache with which it is written. This is not some formulaic panegyric of a great man, but something more relaxed, conversational, accessible. Rowe was in his mid-thirties when he wrote it: a literary man about town, a professional playwright – his edition of Shakespeare was itself a professional undertaking, for which the publisher, Jacob Tonson, paid him £36 10*s* – and a friend of the poet Pope, who spoke warmly of his 'vivacity and gaiety of disposition'. He wrote a series of mellifluous tragedies, one of them, *Jane Shore* (1714), avowedly in imitation of Shakespeare. His most popular play, *The Fair Penitent* (1703), features a serial seducer, the 'haughty, gallant, gay Lothario', whose name remains in the language long after the play has been forgotten. It would be hard to argue that Rowe was anything but a minor author, but he was admired by Dr Johnson, who included him in his *Lives of the Poets*, and who praised the 'suavity' of his style. He was talking of Rowe's plays, but suavity is precisely right as a description of the brisk, fluent tones of the *Account*.

ROWE'S LITERARY CAREER SUGGESTS A KEY feature of this pioneering biography – it is a life of Shakespeare written by a man of the theatre, and drawing on theatrical knowledge and traditions about Shakespeare. An example of this is the casually proffered information that Shakespeare played the part of the Ghost in early productions of *Hamlet*. This wonderful nugget is unique to Rowe, but ties in with an early tradition that Shakespeare played Adam in *As You Like It* –

Opposite: The appearance of the Ghost in Hamlet, *from Rowe's edition. The actor playing Hamlet, with stocking 'down-gyved', is probably Betterton, who appeared in the role for over forty years. His performances drew on traditions and memories of original Shakespearean productions (see p. 16); the over-turned chair, emphasizing Hamlet's shock, may be a piece of stage business created by the first Hamlet, Richard Burbage*

these are smallish parts, and old-man parts, such as a busy, prematurely balding actor-writer might give himself.

A further aspect of this theatrical context is the important contribution made by the veteran actor Thomas Betterton, a colleague of Rowe's who had recently played the title-role in his *Ulysses* (1705). 'I must own a particular obligation to him,' Rowe writes, 'for the most considerable part of the passages relating to [Shakespeare's] Life... his veneration of the memory of Shakespeare having engag'd him to make a journey into Warwickshire, on purpose to gather up what remains he could.' Up in Stratford, Betterton consulted the parish registers and other 'public writings relating to that town'. This is admirable sleuthing by the standards of the day, though in some respects rather carelessly done. It is as well to note now the faulty information which found its way into the *Account*. Shakespeare was not one of ten children but one of eight; and he did not have three daughters, but two daughters and a son. Betterton apparently missed the burial entry for Shakespeare's son, Hamnet, who died in 1596, at the age of eleven. But he did note the details of Shakespeare's marriage, and Rowe is the first biographer to identify the poet's wife – 'the daughter

Thomas Betterton, engraving of 1710 after a portrait by Kneller. The Latin tag – which translates as 'All the world's a stage' – is said to have been the motto of the Globe

of one Hathaway, said to have been a substantial yeoman in the neighbourhood'.

BETTERTON IS NOT TO BE CENSURED, HOWEVER, for the apparent vagueness about Shakespeare's birthdate, which Rowe gives only as 'April, 1564', rather than the traditional 23 April. In this he is more correct than many later biographers. The idea that Shakespeare was born on St George's Day is a jingoistic convenience which was mooted later in the eighteenth century and swiftly became a pseudofact. The only documentary fact is that Shakespeare was baptized on 26 April 1564: the actual day of his birth is unknown. Thomas de Quincey (who was almost as much of a connoisseur of Shakespeare as he was of opium) plausibly suggested that the wedding day of Shakespeare's grand-daughter Elizabeth, 22 April, was chosen in memory of his birthday.

Betterton typifies the lineage of playhouse tradition which lies behind the *Account*. In *Roscius Anglicanus* (1708) John Dennis praised him for his performance in the title-role of Shakespeare and Fletcher's *Henry VIII* – 'the part of the King was so rightly and justly done by Mr Betterton, he being instructed in it by Sir William [Davenant], who had it from old Mr Lowen, that had his instructions from Mr Shakespeare himself' –

Opposite: Frontispiece to Henry VIII *from Rowe's edition. The King – possibly Betterton – and the Cardinal are in historical costume, the set contains a Tudor-like window, and there is even a hint of fan-vaulting about the curtain; but the attendant lords are in 18th-century dress. Unusually, the edge of the stage is shown at the bottom*

The 'Chandos' portrait of Shakespeare, possibly by John Taylor. This is the only portrait of Shakespeare generally accepted as being painted from life

a genealogy akin to the studio lineages of Italian Renaissance painting. Betterton also appears as an early owner of the 'Chandos' portrait of Shakespeare, now in the National Portrait Gallery (above). According to the historian George Vertue, writing in 1719, the then owner of the painting, a barrister named Robert Keck, 'bought [it] for forty guineas off Mr Betterton who bought it of Sir W. Davenant'. Rowe's illustrators were able to use it as the basis of both the frontispiece to each volume (p.28) and the luxury engraving that prefaced the *Account* itself (p.32).

Betterton, born in 1634, had no personal knowledge of Shakespeare, but he was steeped in the texts as a performer. As Rowe says, 'No man is better acquainted with Shakespeare's manner of expression, and indeed he has studied him so well, and is so much a master of him, that whatever part of his he performs, he does it as if it had been written on purpose for him'. The actor who becomes a 'master' of Shakespeare – as we might say, an expert – is a kind of prototype for the biographer, whose mastery of his subject is also to some extent mimetic.

AMONG ROWE'S NOTABLE 'FIRSTS' IS HIS recounting of the story of the young Shakespeare poaching deer from the estates of a Warwickshire grandee, Sir Thomas Lucy of Charlecote. Sometime after his marriage, Rowe says, Shakespeare fell into 'ill Company'. (He married in 1582, so this would have been sometime in his late teens or early twenties.) Among this company were 'some that made a frequent practice of Deer-stealing', who 'engag'd him with them more than once in robbing a Park that belong'd to Sir Thomas Lucy', for which he was 'prosecuted by that Gentleman'. This is one of those stories which sounds like pure folklore, part of the Shakespeare 'mythos', yet it has proved tenacious and even today has its heavyweight proponents. It received an added boost in the 1790s, when Malone found an independent manuscript account, written in the late seventeenth century by an obscure parson named Richard Davies, who said: 'Shakespeare was... much given to all unluckiness in stealing venison & Rabbits particularly from Sr [–] Lucy who had him oft whipt'. This manuscript was hidden away in the archives of Corpus Christi College, Oxford, and it is extremely unlikely that Rowe had read it.

That the story exists in two independent early versions is, of course, no guarantee that it is true, but shows at least that there was a story. Rowe did not invent it. He goes on to note a compelling echo of the case in some badinage from *The Merry Wives of Windsor* (*c.* 1597), where the foolish Justice Shallow accuses Falstaff of poaching from his estates – 'You have... kill'd my deer and broke open my lodge' – and intends to prosecute him for it. Can it be coincidence, Rowe asks, that

A romantic view of the deer-poaching episode, by Joseph Nash, 1839–49

this Shallow is also said to 'give a dozen white luces in the coat' – in other words, to have a family coat of arms featuring luces (young pike), precisely the punning heraldic device used by the Lucys of Charlecote? No commentator on the *Merry Wives* has found a better explanation, and even great modern biographers like E. K. Chambers and Samuel Schoenbaum – doughty documentary empiricists – have felt that the poaching episode as recounted by Rowe has 'the ring of truth'.

ROWE MAKES MUCH OF THIS EPISODE – A SCOOP of sorts – but there is not a whisper of that tediously winsome romanticizing of it found in later, especially Victorian, versions. It is these which provoke scepticism, not the bare bones of the story, which was probably picked up by Betterton in Stratford, where the Lucys were well-known and not especially popular. Throughout Rowe's *Account* there is this judiciousness in his use of biographical material. He states, but does not over-egg, Shakespeare's middling origins, his lack of higher education, his writing by the 'mere light of nature' and so on.

A good deal of Rowe's preface is devoted to critical comment, some of it bearing the imprint of eighteenth century prejudices which today sound quaintly antiquarian. Few, for instance, would agree with his dismissal of tragicomedy as 'the common mistake of that age', since we now value those teasing mood-shifts and plot-twists which the genre brings. But then, to be fair, Rowe does not quite agree with his dismissal, either.

Opposite: Frontispiece to Pericles *from Rowe's edition*

He registers the view, but then adds, 'though the severer critics among us cannot bear it, yet the generality of our audiences seem to be better pleased with it than with an exact tragedy'. Similarly, he is sanguine – as many of those 'severer' critics were not – about Shakespeare's supposed ignorance of the classics. A better knowledge of them might have added more 'correctness' to his style, Rowe thinks, but 'might have restrain'd some of that fire, impetuosity, and even beautiful extravagance which we admire in Shakespeare'.

Some of Rowe's commentary on individual plays seems fluffy and imprecise, but one must set this against the more important and far-reaching precision of his work as an editor. The *Account* introduces the first new edition of the plays since the First Folio. It is an edition which insists on the primacy of Shakespeare's text, but is ready to clarify obvious textual corruptions and fudges with intelligent emendation. In an era when the plays were routinely primped, polished, bowdlerized, rejigged and retitled to accord to ideas of theatrical 'decorum' – Nahum Tate, who rewrote *King Lear* with a happy ending, is the most notorious of these tinkerers, but there were many others – Rowe returns the reader to the original,

Opposite: Frontispiece to King Lear *from Rowe's edition*

difficult, sometimes rough-hewn masterpieces that Shakespeare wrote.

The cheerful, nonchalant quality of Rowe's writing sometimes tends towards the slap-dash, as at the end of the *Account* , where he signs off – or rather, peters out – with a glancing reference to 'a book of [Shakespeare's] Poems publish'd in 1640'. Having only recently got hold of a copy, he adds, 'I won't pretend to determine whether it be his or no'. The edition he refers to, edited by John Benson, is indeed genuine, though textually corrupt: it contains almost all of Shakespeare's sonnets. There may have been some commercial in-fighting behind this dismissal, as a few months later an edition of Shakespeare's poems, based on the 1640 text, was issued by a rival publisher. But that Shakespeare's first biographer could so casually turn aside from this gold-mine of psychological insights into his subject makes one wonder what else Rowe failed to follow up.

For all its faults Rowe's biography has remained durable and readable. There is a modern tendency to dismiss the early biographers as purveyors of unverifiable anecdote and gossip. This seems an arrogant view of writers so much closer to Shakespeare in time, and in cultural context, than we are; writers who simply knew things which we now have to burrow laboriously through ancient archives to rediscover. Dr Johnson notes this point when he describes Rowe's *Account* as 'a life of the author such as tradition, then almost expiring, could supply'. This is what one celebrates three hundred years on – Rowe's timely intervention to rescue a sense of Shakespeare the man, and to preserve some fragments of the shipwreck which might otherwise have been lost forever.

An antiquary admires Shakespeare's monument, by George Vertue, 1737

M:V d^r Gucht Sculp

NOTE ON THE ILLUSTRATIONS

ROWE'S 1709 EDITION OF SHAKESPEARE'S WORKS IS distinguished not only for containing the first biography of Shakespeare, and for its pioneering textual work, but also for being the first illustrated edition. This alone made the edition a landmark in publishing.

Each volume was prefaced with the same image of the poet crowned by Tragedy and Comedy and trumpeted by Fame (reproduced opposite) by a Flemish artist living in London, Michael van der Gucht, copying the French artist Guillaume Vollet. Much more unusually, each play was given its own frontispiece illustrating a particular moment in the action. These illustrations were by a French artist, François Boitard, of whom little is known except that he was in London in 1709, in collaboration with an engraver, Elisha Kirkall, who left a considerable body of work.

There was also, in the more luxurious large paper edition, an elegant version of the 'Chandos'

Opposite: the frontispiece used for each volume of Rowe's edition of Shakespeare. It was copied from a French edition of the works of Corneille, with a version of the 'Chandos' portrait replacing the bust of the French playwright

portrait by the French artist Benoît Arlaud and engraver Gaspard Duchange (p. 32).

Jacob Tonson, the publisher, called the frontispieces to the plays 'cuts' rather than engravings, and this reflects both their lack of sophistication, and their liveliness. There has been disagreement as to how far they illustrate contemporary stage practice, but the answer is surely that while some clearly do – the image of Hamlet overturning his chair in surprise at the appearance of the Ghost is a clear example (p. 13) – others, such as the frontispiece for *The Tempest* (p. 65) are clearly works of pictorial imagination, or, for *Coriolanus* (p. 74), of pictorial appropriation. Still others are a mixture: it is not necessary to decide categorically whether the backgrounds of the frontispieces for *As You Like It* (p. 34), or for *Henry IV Part One* (p. 46), are purely pictorial or a representation of actual theatre scenery; the demeanour of the characters and the general impression are surely close to the stage reality. As such, the prints are not only delightfully varied, but give a vivid picture of the theatre under Queen Anne, with tragic heroes in flowing perukes like Macbeth (p. 69), and Falstaff in his Tudor paunch attacked by Augustan footpads (p. 46). It is the closest we can get to Shakespeare as he was experienced by Dryden or Pope.

The somewhat *ad hoc* approach probably reflects not only a desire for variety, but also time constraints. Tonson was still advertising for information about Shakespeare just two months before publication, and there was certainly no more than two years for the entire project. Only a handful of the plays was performed in that time, so for the majority Boitard could not have drawn on personal memories of the stage. Rowe however, as a consummate man of the theatre, may have been able to supplement with his own knowledge; it seems likely that he at least suggested the choice of scenes. His collaborator, the great actor Betterton, may also have been involved. The awkwardness of some of the more stagey images, and the over-elaboration of others, suggest that Boitard may have been as happy, if not happier, drawing on purely pictorial sources. In any case tight deadlines probably limited the scope for originality – just as they were probably responsible for the copying of the general frontispiece from a French edition of Corneille, and for the signs of haste in the *Account* itself. Tonson recognised both the success and the shortcomings of the cuts by having them redrawn by the more sophisticated Louis du Guernier for the 1714 reprint.

Mr. Wm Shakespear

SOME ACCOUNT OF THE LIFE, &c. OF Mr. *William Shakespear*.

IT SEEMS TO BE A KIND OF RESPECT due to the memory of excellent men, especially of those whom their wit and learning have made famous, to deliver some account of themselves, as well as their works, to posterity. For this reason, how fond do we see some people of discovering any little personal story of the great men of antiquity, their families, the common accidents of their lives, and even their shape, make and features have been the subject of critical enquiries. How trifling soever this curiosity may seem to be, it is certainly very natural; and we are hardly satisfied with an account of any remarkable person, till we have heard him described even to the very clothes he wears. As for what relates to men of letters, the knowledge of an author may sometimes conduce to the better understanding his book: and though the works of Mr. Shakespeare may seem to many not to want a comment, yet I fancy some little account of the man himself may not be thought improper to go along with them.

He was the son of Mr. John Shakespeare, and was born at Stratford upon Avon, in Warwickshire, in April 1564. His family, as appears by the register and public writings relating to that town,

Opposite: Frontispiece to As You Like It, *from Rowe's edition*

were of good figure and fashion there, and are mentioned as gentlemen. His father, who was a considerable dealer in wool, had so large a family, ten children in all,* that though he was his eldest son, he could give him no better education than his own employment. He had bred him, 'tis true, for some time at a Free School,† where 'tis probable he aquired that little Latin he was master of; but the narrowness of his circumstances, and the want of his assistance at home, forced his father to withdraw him from thence, and unhappily prevented his further proficiency in that language. It is without controversy, that he had no knowledge of the writings of the ancient poets, not only from this reason, but from his works themselves, where we find no traces of anything that looks like an imitation of them; the delicacy of his taste, and the natural bent of his own great genius, equal, if not superior to some of the best of theirs, would certainly have led him to read and study them with so much pleasure, that some of their fine images would naturally have insinuated themselves into, and been mixed with his own writings; so that his not copying at least something from them, may be an argument

* In fact eight, of whom two died in infancy.

† Almost certainly the Grammar School of King Edward VI

of his never having read them. Whether his ignorance of the ancients were a disadvantage to him or no, may admit of a dispute: for though the knowledge of them might have made him more correct, yet it is not improbable but that the regularity and deference for them, which would have attended that correctness, might have restrained some of that fire, impetuosity, and even beautiful extravagance which we admire in Shakespeare. And I believe we are better pleased with those thoughts, altogether new and uncommon, which his own imagination supplied him so abundantly with, than if he had given us the most beautiful passages out of the Greek and Latin poets, and that in the most agreeable manner that it was possible for a master of the English language to deliver them. Some Latin without question he did know, and one may see up and down in his plays how far his reading that way went. In *Love's Labour Lost*, the Pedant comes out with a verse of Mantuan [Virgil]; and in *Titus Andronicus*, one of the Gothic princes, upon reading

> Integer vitæ scelerisque purus
> Non eget Mauri jaculis nec arcu*

* *Titus Andronicus* IV, ii, 20–21. 'The man of upright life and free from crime does not need the javelins or bows of the Moor.' Horace, Ode 22.

The earliest drawing of a Shakespearean performance:
Titus Andronicus, *sketched in c. 1595*

says, *'Tis a verse in Horace, but he remembers it out of his Grammar*: which, I suppose, was the author's case.* Whatever Latin he had, 'tis certain he understood French, as may be observed from many words and sentences scattered up and down his plays in that language; and especially from one scene in *Henry V* written wholly in it. Upon his leaving school, he seems to have given entirely into that way of living which his father proposed to him; and in order to settle in the world after a family manner, he thought fit to marry while he was yet very young. His wife was the daughter of one Hathaway, said to have been a substantial yeoman in the neighbourhood of Stratford. In this kind of settlement he continued for some time,

* The 'Grammar' is Lily's Latin grammar, *Brevissima Institutio*, the authorised textbook in English schools from 1542

till an extravagance that he was guilty of, forced him both out of his country and that way of living which he had taken up; and though it seemed at first to be a blemish upon his good manners, and a misfortune to him, yet it afterwards happily proved the occasion of exerting one of the greatest geniuses that ever was known in dramatic poetry. He had, by a misfortune common enough to young fellows, fallen into ill company; and amongst them, some that made a frequent practice of deer-stealing, engaged him with them more than once in robbing a park that belonged to Sir Thomas Lucy of Charlecote, near Stratford. For this he was prosecuted by that gentleman, as he thought, somewhat too severely; and in order to revenge that ill usage, he made a ballad upon him. And though this, probably the first essay of his poetry, be lost, yet it is said to have been so very bitter, that it redoubled the prosecution against him to that degree, that he was obliged to leave his business and family in Warwickshire, for some time, and shelter himself in London.

It is at this time, and upon this accident, that

Overleaf: detail from Wenceslaus Hollar's 'Long View' of London, etched in 1647 but closer than any other image to the city that Shakespeare knew. The building marked 'Beere bayting' is in fact the Globe (as rebuilt after the fire of 1613); the one marked 'Globe' is the Hope Theatre, which replaced the bear baiting building in 1614

New Exchange
Convent garden
S. Clement
Arundel house
The Globe

S. Pauwls Church
S. y^e Waterhouse
S. Andre in Holborne
Heygat
Paulus wharfe
Queene hythe
The 3. Cranes
the Eel Ships
T H A M E
Winchester house

he is said to have made his first acquaintance in the playhouse. He was received into the company then in being, at first in a very mean rank; but his admirable wit, and the natural turn of it to the stage, soon distinguished him, if not as an extraordinary actor, yet as an excellent writer. His name is printed, as the custom was in those times, amongst those of the other players, before some old plays, but without any particular account of what sort of parts he used to play; and though I have inquired, I could never meet with any further account of him this way, than that the top of his performance was the Ghost in his own *Hamlet*. I should have been much more pleased, to have learned from some certain authority, which was the first play he wrote; it would be without doubt a pleasure to any man, curious in things of this kind, to see and know what was the first essay of a fancy like Shakespeare's. Perhaps we are not to look for his beginnings, like those of other authors, among their least perfect writings; art had so little, and nature so large a share in what he did, that, for aught I know, the performances of his youth, as they were the most vigorous, and had the most fire and strength of imagination in them, were the best. I would not be thought by this to mean, that his fancy was so loose and

The only surviving contemporaraneous drawing of the interior of an Elizabethan playhouse: the Swan, sketched in 1596 by a Dutch visitor, Johannes de Witt, who describes it as 'the largest and most magnificent... for it accommodates in its seats three thousand persons'. Steps on either side (labelled 'ingressus' *on the left), lead to the yard dominated by the stage (*'proscænium'*); behind stands the tiring house (*'mimorum ædes'*), where the actors change costumes and store props; on the first floor are boxes with spectators, or perhaps musicians. A man blowing a trumpet with a swan banner stands in the attic, which could also be used for flying effects*

extravagant, as to be independent on the rule and government of judgment; but that what he thought, was commonly so great, so justly and rightly conceived in itself, that it wanted little or no correction, and was immediately approved by an impartial judgment at the first sight. Mr. Dryden seems to think that *Pericles* is one of his first plays; but there is no judgment to be formed on that, since there is good reason to believe that the greatest part of that play was not written by him; though it is owned, some part of it certainly was, particularly the last act. But though the order of time in which the several pieces were written be generally uncertain, yet there are passages in some few of them which seem to fix their dates. So the Chorus in the beginning of the fifth act of *Henry V* by a compliment very handsomely turned to the Earl of Essex, shows the play to have been written when that lord was general for the Queen in Ireland: and his Elegy upon Queen Elizabeth, and her successor King James, in the latter end of his *Henry VIII*, is a proof of that play's being written after the accession of the latter of those two princes to the crown of England. Whatever the particular times of his writing were, the people of his age, who began to grow wonderfully fond of diversions of this kind, could not but be highly pleased to see a genius arise amongst them of so pleasurable, so rich a vein, and so plentifully capable of furnishing their favourite entertainments. Besides the advantages of his wit, he was in himself a good-natured man, of great sweetness in his manners, and a most agreeable companion; so that it is no wonder if with so many good qualities he made himself acquainted with the best conversations of those times. Queen Elizabeth had several of his plays acted before her, and without doubt gave him many gracious marks of her favour. It is that maiden princess plainly, whom he intends by

> A fair vestal, throned by the west.*

And that whole passage is a compliment very properly brought in, and very handsomely applied to her. She was so well pleased with that admirable character of Falstaff, in the two parts of *Henry the Fourth*, that she commanded him to continue it for one play more, and to show him in love. This is said to be the occasion of his writing *The Merry Wives of Windsor*. How well she was obeyed, the play itself is an admirable proof. Upon this occasion it may not be improper to observe, that

* *A Midsummer Night's Dream*, II, i, 161

this part of Falstaff is said to have been written originally under the name of Oldcastle; some of that family being then remaining, the Queen was pleased to command him to alter it; upon which he made use of Falstaff. The present offence was indeed avoided; but I don't know whether the author may not have been somewhat to blame in his second choice, since it is certain that Sir John Falstaff, who was a Knight of the Garter, and a lieutenant-general, was a name of distinguished merit in the wars in France in Henry the Fifth's and Henry the Sixth's times.

What grace soever the Queen conferred upon him, it was not to her only he owed the fortune which the reputation of his wit made. He had the honour to meet with many great and uncommon marks of favour and friendship from the Earl of Southampton, famous in the histories of that time for his friendship to the unfortunate Earl of Essex. It was to that noble lord that he dedicated his *Venus and Adonis*, the only piece of his poetry which he ever published himself,* though many of his plays were surreptitiously and lamely printed

* Rowe forgets *The Rape of Lucrece*, published in 1594 and also dedicated to Southampton; and the *Sonnets*, published in 1609

Opposite: Falstaff at Gad's Hill, beaten by Prince Hal and Poins in buckram masks, frontispiece to First Part of Henry IV *in Rowe's edition. The actor playing Falstaff is likely to be Thomas Betterton*

in his lifetime. There is one instance so singular in the magnificence of this patron of Shakespeare's, that if I had not been assured that the story was handed down by Sir William Davenant, who was probably very well acquainted with his affairs,* I should not have ventured to have inserted, that my Lord Southampton, at one time, gave him a thousand pounds, to enable him to go through with a purchase which he heard he had a mind to. A bounty very great, and very rare at any time, and almost equal to that profuse generosity the present age has shown to French dancers and Italian eunuchs.

What particular habitude or friendship he contracted with private men, I have not been able to learn, more than that every one who had a true taste of merit, and could distinguish men, had generally a just value and esteem for him. His exceeding candour and good nature must certainly have inclined all the gentler part of the world to love him, as the power of his wit obliged the men of the most delicate knowledge and polite learning to admire him. Amongst these was the incomparable Mr. Edmund Spenser, who speaks of him in his *Tears of the Muses*, not only with the

* Davenant claimed, with some plausibility, to be Shakespeare's natural son

praises due to a good poet, but even lamenting his absence with the tenderness of a friend. The passage is in Thalia's complaint for the decay of dramatic poetry, and the contempt the stage then lay under, amongst his miscellaneous works.

> And he the man, whom Nature's self had made
> To mock her self, and Truth to imitate
> With kindly counter under mimic shade,
> Our pleasant Willy, ah! is dead of late:
> With whom all joy and jolly merriment
> Is also deaded, and in dolour drent.
>
> Instead thereof, scoffing scurrility
> And scorning folly with contempt is crept,
> Rolling in rhymes of shameless ribaldry,
> Without regard or due decorum kept;
> Each idle wit at will presumes to make,
> And doth the learned's task upon him take.
>
> But that same gentle spirit, from whose pen
> Large streams of honey and sweet nectar flow,
> Scorning the boldness of such base-born men,
> Which dare their follies forth so rashly throw;
> Doth rather choose to sit in idle cell,
> Than so himself to mockery to sell.

I know some people have been of the opinion, that Shakespeare is not meant by *Willy* in the first stanza of these verses, because Spenser's death happened twenty years before Shakespeare's.* But, besides that the character is not applicable to any man of that time but himself, it is plain by the last stanza that Mr. Spenser does not mean that he was then really dead, but only that he had withdrawn himself from the public, or at least withheld his hand from writing, out of a disgust he had taken at the then ill taste of the town, and the mean condition of the stage. Mr. Dryden was always of opinion these verses were meant of Shakespeare; and 'tis highly probable they were so, since he was three and thirty years old at Spenser's death; and his reputation in poetry must have been great enough before that time to have deserved what is here said of him.

His acquaintance with Ben Jonson began with a remarkable piece of humanity and good nature. Mr. Jonson, who was at that time altogether unknown to the world, had offered one of his plays to the players, in order to have it acted; and the persons into whose hands it was put, after having turned it carelessly and superciliously over, were just upon returning it to him with an ill-natured answer, that it would be of no service to their

* Spenser's reference in *The Tears of the Muses* (1590) is now thought to be more probably to Richard Wills or Willey, author of *De Re Poetica*

company, when Shakespeare luckily cast his eye upon it, and found something so well in it as to engage him first to read it through, and afterwards to recommend Mr. Jonson and his writings to the public. After this they were professed friends; though I don't know whether the other ever made him an equal return of gentleness and sincerity. Ben was naturally proud and insolent, and in the days of his reputation did so far take upon him the supremacy in wit, that he could not but look with an evil eye upon any one that seemed to stand in competition with him. And if at times he has affected to commend him, it has always been with some reserve, insinuating his uncorrectness, a careless manner of writing, and want of judgment; the praise of seldom altering or blotting out what he writ, which was given him by the players who were the first publishers of his works after his death, was what Jonson could not bear; he thought it impossible, perhaps, for another man to strike out the greatest thoughts in the finest expression, and to reach those excellencies of poetry with the ease of a first imagination, which himself with infinite labour and study could but hardly attain to. Jonson was certainly a very good scholar, and in that had the advantage of Shakespeare; though at the same time I believe it must be allowed, that what nature gave the latter, was more than a balance for what books had given the former; and judgment of a great man upon this occasion was, I think, very just and proper. In a conversation between Sir John Suckling, Sir William Davenant, Endymion Porter, Mr. Hales of Eaton, and Ben Jonson, Sir John Suckling, who was a professed admirer of Shakespeare had undertaken his defence against Ben Jonson with some warmth. Mr. Hales, who had sat still for some time, hearing Ben frequently reproaching him with the want of learning, and ignorance of the ancients, told him at last, *That if Mr. Shakespeare had not read the ancients, he had likewise not stolen any thing from 'em;* (a fault the other made no conscience of) *and that if he would produce any one topic finely treated by any of them, he would undertake to show something upon the same subject at least as well written by Shakespeare.* Jonson did indeed take a large liberty, even to the transcribing and translating of whole scenes together; and sometimes, with all deference to so great a name as his, not altogether for the advantage of the authors of whom he borrowed. And if Augustus and Virgil were really what he has made them in a scene of his *Poetaster*, they are as odd an emperor and a poet as ever met.

Shakespeare, on the other hand, was beholding to no body farther than the foundation of the tale, the incidents were often his own, and the writing entirely so. There is one play of his, indeed, *The Comedy of Errors*, in a great measure taken from the *Menæchmi* of Plautus. How that happened, I cannot easily divine, since, as I hinted before, I do not take him to have been master of Latin enough to read it in the original, and I know of no translation of Plautus so old as his time.*

As I have not proposed to myself to enter into a large and complete criticism upon Mr. Shakespeare's works, so I suppose it will neither be expected that I should take notice of the severe remarks that have been formerly made upon him by Mr. Rhymer.† I must confess, I can't very well see what could be the reason of his animadverting with so much sharpness, upon the faults of a man excellent on most occasions, and whom all the world ever was and will be inclined to have an esteem and veneration for. If it was to show his own knowledge in the art of poetry, besides that there is a vanity in making that only his design,

* One was in fact published in 1595, the year after *The Comedy of Errors* was performed, but may have been previously available to Shakespeare in manuscript

† Thomas Rhymer in *A Short View of Tragedy*, published in 1693

I question if there be not many imperfections as well in those schemes and precepts he has given for the direction of others, as well as in that sample of tragedy which he has written to show the excellence of his own genius. If he had a pique against the man, and wrote on purpose to ruin a reputation so well established, he has had the mortification to fail altogether in his attempt, and to see the world at least as fond of Shakespeare as of his critic. But I won't believe a gentleman, and a good natured man, capable of the last intention. Whatever may have been his meaning, finding fault is certainly the easiest task of knowledge, and commonly those men of good judgment, who are likewise of good and gentle dispositions, abandon this ungrateful province to the tyranny of pedants. If one would enter into the beauties of Shakespeare, there is a much larger, as well as a more delightful field; but as I won't prescribe to the tastes of other people, so I will only take the liberty, with all due submissions to the judgment of others, to observe some of those things I have been pleased with in looking him over.

His plays are properly to be distinguished only into comedies and tragedies. Those which are called histories, and even some of his comedies, are really tragedies, with a run or mixture of comedy amongst them. That way of tragi-comedy was the common mistake of that age, and is indeed become so agreeable to the English taste, that though the severer critiques among us cannot bear it, yet the generality of our audiences seem to be better pleased with it than with an exact tragedy. *The Merry Wives of Windsor*, *The Comedy of Errors*, and *The Taming of the Shrew* are all pure comedy; the rest, however they are called, have something of both kinds. 'Tis not very easy to determine which way of writing he was most excellent in. There is certainly a great deal of entertainment in his comical humours; and though they did not then strike at all ranks of people, as the satire of the present age has taken the liberty to do, yet there is a pleasing and a well distinguished variety in those characters which he thought fit to meddle with. Falstaff is allowed by everybody to be a masterpiece; the character is always well sustained, though drawn out into the length of three plays; and even the account of his death, given by his old landlady Mrs. Quickly, in the first act of *Henry V*, though it be extremely natural, is yet as diverting as any part of his life. If there be any fault in the draught he has made of this lewd old fellow, it is, that though he has made him a thief, lying, cowardly, vainglorious, and in short every way vicious, yet he has given him so much wit as to make him almost too agreeable; and I don't know whether some people have not, in remembrance of the diversion he had formerly afforded them, been sorry to see his friend Hal use him so scurvily, when he comes to the crown in the end of the *Second Part of Henry the Fourth*. Amongst other extravagances, in *The Merry Wives of Windsor*, he has made him a deer-stealer, that he might at the same time remember his Warwickshire prosecutor, under the name of Justice Shallow; he has given him very near the same coat of arms which Dugdale, in his *Antiquities* of that county, describes for a family there, and makes the Welsh parson descant very pleasantly upon them. That whole play is admirable; the humours are various and well opposed; the main design, which is to cure Ford of his unreasonable jealousy, is extremely well conducted. Falstaff's billet-doux, and Master Slender's

Ah! Sweet Ann Page!

are very good expressions of love in their way. In *Twelfth Night* there is something singularly ridiculous and pleasant in the fantastical steward Malvolio. The parasite and the vain-glorious

Opposite: Frontispiece to Twelfth Night, *from Rowe's edition*

in Parolles, in *All's Well that ends Well*, is as good as any thing of that kind in Plautus or Terence. Petruchio, in *The Taming of the Shrew*, is an uncommon piece of humour. The conversation of Benedick and Beatrice, in *Much Ado about Nothing*, and of Rosalind in *As You Like It*, have much wit and sprightliness all along. His clowns, without which character there was hardly any play writ in that time, are all very entertaining; and, I believe, Thersites in *Troilus and Cressida*, and Apemantus in *Timon*, will be allowed to be masterpieces of ill nature, and satirical snarling. To these I might add, that incomparable character of Shylock the Jew, in *The Merchant of Venice*; but though we have seen that play received and acted as a comedy, and the part of the Jew performed by an excellent comedian, yet I cannot but think it was designed tragically by the author. There appears in it such a deadly spirit of revenge, such a savage fierceness and fellness, and such a bloody designation of cruelty and mischief, as cannot agree either with the style or characters of comedy. The play itself, take it all together, seems to me to be one of the most finished of any Shakespeare's. The tale indeed, in that part relating to the caskets, and the

Opposite: Frontispiece to The Taming of the Shrew, *from Rowe's edition*

extravagant and unusual kind of bond given by Antonio, is a little too much removed from the rules of probability: but taking the fact for granted, we must allow it to be very beautifully written. There is something in the friendship of Antonio and Bassanio very great, generous and tender. The whole fourth act, supposing, as I said, the fact to be probable, is extremely fine. But there are two passages that deserve a particular notice. The first is, what Portia says in praise of mercy [IV, i, 182-203]; and the other on the power of music [V, i, 83-88]. The melancholy of Jaques, in *As You Like It*, is as singular and odd as it is diverting. And if what Horace says *Difficile est proprie communia dicere*,* 'twill be be a hard task for any one to go beyond him in the description of the several degrees and ages of man's life, though the thought be old, and common enough.

All the world's a stage;
And all the men and women merely players;
They have their exits and their entrances,
And one man in his time plays many parts,
His acts being seven ages. At first the infant
Mewling and puking in the nurse's arms:

* *Ars Poetica*, 128. 'It is hard to treat in your own way what is common.'

Opposite: Frontispiece to The Merchant of Venice, *from Rowe's edition*

And then, the whining school-boy with his satchel,
And shining morning-face, creeping like snail
Unwillingly to school. And then the lover
Sighing like furnace, with a woeful ballad
Made to his mistress' eye-brow. Then a soldier
Full of strange oaths, and bearded like the pard,
Jealous in honour, sudden and quick in quarrel,
Seeking the bubble reputation
Ev'n in the cannon's mouth. And then the Justice
In fair round belly, with good capon lined,
With eyes severe, and beard of formal cut,
Full of wise saws and modern instances;
And so he plays his part. The sixth age shifts
Into the lean and slippered pantaloon,
With spectacles on nose, and pouch on side;
His youthful hose, well saved, a world too wide
For his shrunk shank; and his big manly voice
Turning again tow'rd childish treble pipes,
And whistles in his sound. Last scene of all,
That ends this strange eventful history,
Is second childishness and mere oblivion,
Sans teeth, sans eyes, sans taste, sans everything.*

His images are indeed everywhere so lively, that the thing he would represent stands full before you, and you possess every part of it. I will venture to point out one more, which is, I think, as strong and as uncommon as any thing I ever

* *As You Like It,* II, 7, 139–166

saw; 'tis an image of Patience. Speaking of a maid in love, he says,

> She never told her love,
> But let concealment, like a worm i' th' bud
> Feed on her damask cheek: She pined
>   in thought, [...]
> And sat like Patience on a monument,
> Smiling at grief.*

What an image is here given! and what a task would it have been for the greatest masters of Greece and Rome to have expressed the passions designed by this sketch of statuary? The style of his comedy is, in general, natural to the characters, and easy in itself; and the wit most commonly sprightly and pleasing, except in those places where he runs into doggerel rhymes, as in *The Comedy of Errors*, and a passage or two in some other plays. As for his jingling sometimes, and playing upon words, it was the common vice of the age he lived in: and if we find it in the pulpit, made use of as an ornament to the sermons of some of the gravest divines of those times, perhaps it may not be thought too light for the stage.

But certainly the greatness of this author's genius does nowhere so much appear, as where he

* *Twelfth Night*, II, 4, 113–118

gives his imagination an entire loose, and raises his fancy to a flight above mankind and the limits of the visible world. Such are his attempts in *The Tempest*, *Midsummer-Night's Dream*, *Macbeth* and *Hamlet*. Of these, *The Tempest*, however it comes to be placed the first by the former publishers of his works, can never have been the first written by him: it seems to me as perfect in its kind, as almost any thing we have of his. One may observe, that the unities are kept here with an exactness uncommon to the liberties of his writing: though that was what, I suppose, he valued himself least upon, since his excellencies were all of another kind. I am very sensible that he does, in this play, depart too much from that likeness to truth which ought to be observed in these sort of writings; yet he does it so very finely, that one is easily drawn in to have more faith for his sake, than reason does well allow of. His magic has something in it very solemn and very poetical; and that extravagant character of Caliban is mighty well sustained, shows a wonderful invention in the author, who could strike out such a particular wild image, and is certainly one of the finest and

Opposite: Frontispiece to The Tempest, *from Rowe's edition. Prospero on his island in the distance unleashes the elements and spirits; Ariel twists the boat by the mainmast*

most uncommon grotesques that was ever seen. The observation, which I have been informed three very great men* concurred in making upon this part, was extremely just: *that Shakespeare had not only found out a new character in his Caliban but had also devised and adapted a new manner of language for that character*. Among the particular beauties of this piece, I think one may be allowed to point out the tale of Prospero in the first act; his speech to Ferdinand in the fourth, upon the breaking up the masque of Juno and Ceres; and that in the fifth, where he dissolves his charms, and resolves to break his magic rod. This play has been altered by Sir William Davenant and Mr. Dryden; and though I won't arraign the judgment of those two great men, yet I think I may be allowed to say, that there are some things left out by them, that might, and even ought to have been kept in. Mr. Dryden was an admirer of our author, and, indeed, he owed him a great deal, as those who have read them both may very easily observe. And, I think, in justice to them both, I should not on this occasion omit what Mr. Dryden has said of him:

* Rowe identifies these as the author Lucius Cary, 2nd Viscount Falkland; the Lord Chief Justice, Sir John Vaughan; and the polymath John Selden

Shakespeare, who, taught by none, did first impart
To Fletcher wit, to lab'ring Jonson art.
He, monarch-like, gave those his subjects law,
And is that nature which they paint and draw.
Fletcher reached that which on his heights did grow,
Whilst Jonson crept and gathered all below:
This did his love, and this his mirth digest,
One imitates him most, the other best.
If they have since out-writ all other men,
'Tis with the drops which fell from Shakespeare's
pen.
The storm which vanished on the neighb'ring shore,
Was taught by Shakespeare's Tempest first to roar.
That innocence and beauty which did smile
In Fletcher, grew on this enchanted isle.
But Shakespeare's magic could not copied be,
Within that circle none durst walk but he.
I must confess 'twas bold, nor would you now
That liberty to vulgar wits allow,
Which works by magic supernatural things:
But Shakespeare's pow'r is sacred as a king's.

Prologue to *The Tempest*, as it is altered
by Mr. Dryden

It is the same magic that raises the fairies in *Midsummer Night's Dream*, the witches in *Macbeth*, and the Ghost in *Hamlet*, with thoughts and language so proper to the parts they sustain, and so peculiar to the talent of this writer. But of the two last of these plays I shall have occasion to take notice, among the tragedies of Mr. Shakespeare. If one undertook to examine the greatest part of these by those rules which are established by Aristotle, and taken from the model of the Grecian stage, it would be no very hard task to find a great many faults. But as Shakespeare lived under a kind of mere light of nature, and had never been made acquainted with the regularity of those written precepts, so it would be hard to judge him by a law he knew nothing of. We are to consider him as a man that lived in a state of almost universal license and ignorance: there was no established judge, but every one took the liberty to write according to the dictates of his own fancy. When one considers, that there is not one play before him of a reputation good enough to entitle it to an appearance on the present stage, it cannot but be a matter of great wonder that he should advance dramatic poetry so far as he did. The fable is what is generally placed the first, among those that are reckoned the constituent parts of a tragic or heroic poem; not, perhaps, as it is the most difficult or

Opposite: The witches show Macbeth the line of kings descended from Banquo, who walks behind them; frontispiece to Rowe's edition

beautiful, but as it is the first properly to be thought of in the contrivance and course of the whole; and with the fable ought to be considered, the fit disposition, order and conduct of its several parts. As it is not in this province of the drama that the strength and mastery of Shakespeare lay, so I shall not undertake the tedious and ill-natured trouble to point out the several faults he was guilty of in it. His tales were seldom invented, but rather taken either from true history, or novels and romances; and he commonly made use of them in that order, with those incidents, and that extent of time in which he found them in the authors from whence he borrowed them. So *The Winter's Tale*, which is taken from an old book called *The Delectable History of Dorastus and Faunia*, contains the space of sixteen or seventeen years, and the scene is sometimes laid in Bohemia, and sometimes in Sicily, according to the original order of the story. Almost all his historical plays comprehend a great length of time, and very different and distinct places, and in his *Antony and Cleopatra*, the scene travels over the greatest part of the Roman Empire. But in recompense for his carelessness in this point, when he comes to another part of the drama, the manners of his characters, in acting or speaking what is proper for them, and fit to be shown by the poet, he may be generally justified, and in very many places greatly commended. For those plays which he has taken from the English or Roman history, let any man compare them, and he will find the character as exact in the poet as the historian. He seems indeed so far from proposing to himself any one action for a subject, that the title very often tells you, 'tis *The Life of King John, King Richard*, &c. What can be more agreeable to the idea our historians give of Henry the Sixth, than the picture Shakespeare has drawn of him! His manners are everywhere exactly the same with the story; one finds him still described with simplicity, passive sanctity, want of courage, weakness of mind, and easy submission to the governance of an imperious wife, or prevailing faction, though at the same time the poet does justice to his good qualities, and moves the pity of his audience for him, by showing him pious, disinterested, a contemner of things of this world, and wholly resigned to the severest dispensations of God's providence. There is a short scene in the *Second Part of Henry VI*, which I cannot but think admirable in its kind. Cardinal Beaufort, who had murdered the Duke of Gloucester, is shown in the last agonies on his death-bed, with the good King praying over him.

There is so much terror in one, so much tenderness and moving piety in the other, as must touch any one who is capable either of fear or pity. In his *Henry VIII* that prince is drawn with that greatness of mind, and all those good qualities which are attributed to him in any account of his reign. If his faults are not shown in an equal degree, and the shades in this picture do not bear a just proportion to the lights, it is not that the artist wanted either colours or skill in the disposition of them; but the truth, I believe, might be, that he forbore doing it out of regard to Queen Elizabeth, since it could have been no very great respect to the memory of his mistress to have exposed some certain parts of her father's life upon the stage. He has dealt much more freely with the minister of that great king, and certainly nothing was ever more justly written, than the character of Cardinal Wolsey. He has shown him tyrannical, cruel, and insolent in his prosperity; and yet, by a wonderful address, he makes his fall and ruin the subject of general compassion. The whole man, with his vices and virtues, is finely

Opposite: Death of Cardinal Beaufort, frontispiece to The Second Part of Henry VI, *from Rowe's edition. The use of this scene (III, 3) for the frontispiece suggests that Rowe was consulted for the illustrations*

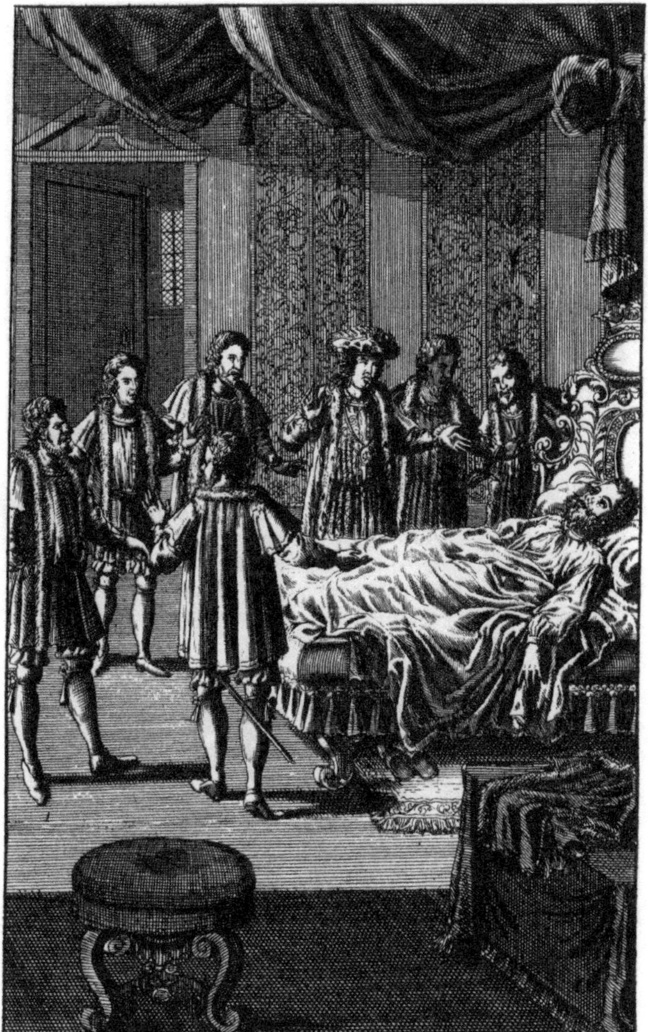

and exactly described in the second scene of the fourth act. The distresses likewise of Queen Katherine, in this play, are very movingly touched; and though the art of the poet has screened King Henry from any gross imputation of injustice, yet one is inclined to wish, the Queen had met with a fortune more worthy of her birth and virtue. Nor are the manners proper to the persons represented less justly observed in those characters taken from the Roman history; and of this, the fierceness and impatience of Coriolanus, his courage and disdain of the common people, the virtue and philosophical temper of Brutus, the irregular greatness of mind in Mark Antony, are beautiful proofs. For the two last especially, you find them exactly as they are described by Plutarch, from whom certainly Shakespeare copied them. He has indeed followed his original pretty close, and taken in several little incidents that might have been spared in a play. But, as I hinted before, his design seems most commonly rather to describe those great men in the several fortunes and accidents of their lives, than to take any single great action, and form his work simply

Opposite: Coriolanus being entreated by his family, frontispiece from Rowe's edition. Unlike most of the frontispieces, this is based not on a stage setting but on a painting by Poussin

upon that. However, there are some of his pieces, where the fable is founded upon one action only. Such are more especially, *Romeo and Juliet*, *Hamlet*, and *Othello*. The design in *Romeo and Juliet*, is plainly the punishment of their two families, for the unreasonable feuds and animosities that had been so long kept up between them, and occasioned the effusion of so much blood. In the management of this story, he has shown something wonderfully tender and passionate in the love-part, and very pitiful in the distress. *Hamlet* is founded on much the same tale with the *Electra* of Sophocles. In each of them a young prince is engaged to revenge the death of his father, their mothers are equally guilty, are both concerned in the murder of their husbands, and are afterwards married to the murderers. There is in the first part of the Greek tragedy, something very moving in the grief of Electra; but as Mr. D'Acier* has observed, there is something very unnatural and shocking in the manners he has given that princess and Orestes in the latter part. Orestes embrues his hands in the blood of his own mother; and that barbarous action is perfomed, though

* André Dacier, French classicist

Opposite: The death of Juliet, frontispiece from Rowe's edition of Romeo and Juliet

not immediately upon the stage, yet so near, that the audience hear Clytemnestra crying out to Ægisthus for help, and to her son for mercy, while Electra, her daughter, and a princess, both of them characters that ought to have appeared with more decency, stands upon the stage and encourages her brother in the parricide. What horror does this not raise! Clytemnestra was a wicked woman, and had deserved to die; nay, in the truth of the story, she was killed by her own son; but to represent an action of this kind on the stage, is certainly an offence against those rules of manners proper to the persons that ought to be observed there. On the contrary, let us only look a little on the conduct of Shakespeare. Hamlet is represented with the same piety towards his father, and resolution to revenge his death, as Orestes; he has the same abhorrence for his mother's guilt, which, to provoke him the more, is heightened by incest. But 'tis with wonderful art and justness of judgment, that the poet restrains him from doing violence to his mother. To prevent anything of that kind, he makes his father's ghost forbid that part of his vengeance.

> But howsoever thou pursu'st this act,
> Taint not thy mind; nor let thy soul contrive
> Against thy mother aught; leave her to Heav'n,

And to those thorns that in her bosom lodge,
To prick and sting her.*

This is to distinguish rightly between *horror* and *terror*. The latter is a proper passion of tragedy, but the former ought always to be carefully avoided. And certainly no dramatic writer ever succeeded better in raising terror in the minds of an audience than Shakespeare has done. The whole tragedy of *Macbeth*, but more especially the scene where the King is murdered, in the second act, as well as this play, is noble proof of that manly spirit with which he writ; and both show how powerful he was, in giving the strongest motions to our souls that they are capable of.

I cannot leave *Hamlet*, without taking notice of the advantage with which we have seen this masterpiece of Shakespeare distinguish itself upon the stage, by Mr. Betterton's fine performance of that part. A man, who though he had no other good qualities, as he has a great many, must have made his way into the esteem of all men of letters, by this only excellency. No man is better acquainted with Shakespeare's manner of expression, and indeed he has studied him so well, and is so much a master of him, that whatever part of his he

* *Hamlet*, 1, 5, 84-88

performs, he does it as if it had been written on purpose for him, and that the author had exactly conceived it as he plays it. I must own a particular obligation to him, for the most considerable part of the passages relating to his life, which I have here transmitted to the public; his veneration for the memory of Shakespeare having engaged him to make a journey into Warwickshire, on purpose to gather up what remains he could of a name for which he had so great a value.

Since I had at first resolved not to enter into any critical controversy, I won't pretend to enquire into the justness of Mr. Rhymer's remarks on *Othello*; he has certainly pointed out some faults very judiciously; and indeed they are such as most people will agree, with him, to be faults. But I wish he would likewise have observed some of the beauties too, as I think it became an exact and equal critic to do. It seems strange that he should allow nothing good in the whole: if the fable and incidents are not to his taste, yet the thoughts are almost every where very noble, and the diction manly and proper. These last, indeed, are parts of Shakespeare's praise, which it would be very hard to dispute with him. His sentiments and images of things are great and natural; and

Opposite: Frontispiece to Othello *from Rowe's edition*

his expression (though perhaps in some instances a little irregular) just, and raised in proportion to his subject and occasion. It would be even endless to mention the particular instances that might be given of this kind. But his book is in the possession of the public, and 'twill be hard to dip into any part of it, without finding what I have said of him made good.

The latter part of his life was spent, as all men of good sense will wish theirs may be, in ease, retirement, and the conversation of his friends. He had the good fortune to gather an estate equal to his occasion, and, in that, to his wish; and is said to have spent some years before his death at his native Stratford. His pleasurable wit, and good nature, engaged him in the acquaintance, and entitled him to the friendship of the gentlemen of the neighbourhood. Amongst them, it is a story almost still remembered in that country, that he had a particular intimacy with Mr. Combe, an old gentleman noted thereabouts for his wealth and usury. It happened, that in a pleasant conversation amongst their common friends, Mr. Combe told Shakespeare in a laughing manner, that he fancied, he intended to write his epitaph, if he happened to outlive him; and since he could not know what might be said of him when he was dead, he desired it might be done immediately. Upon which Shakespeare gave him these four verses:

Ten in the hundred lies here engraved,
'Tis a hundred to ten, his soul is not saved:
If any Man ask, who lies in this tomb?
Oh! ho! quoth the Devil, 'tis my John-a-Combe.

But the sharpness of the satire is said to have stung the man so severely, that he never forgave it.*

He died in the 53d year of his age, and was buried on the north side of the chancel, in the great church at Stratford, where a monument, as engraved in the plate, is placed in the wall. On his gravestone underneath is:

Good Friend, for Jesus sake, forbear
To dig the Dust inclosed here.
Blest be the Man that spares these Stones,
And Curst be he that moves my Bones.

He had three daughters,† of which two lived to be married; Judith, the elder, to one Mr. Thomas Quiney, by whom she had three sons, who all died without children; and Susannah, who was his

* In fact Combe left Shakespeare the sizeable sum of £5

† In fact two daughters and a son; Susannah was the eldest, born 1583, and Judith and Hamnet were twins, born 1585

Shakespeare's tomb, as illustrated in Rowe's Life. *This is a not very accurate representation based on Dugdale's* Antiquities; *in particular it omits the pen, making Shakespeare more of a wool merchant than a poet. Of the epitaph only the Latin verses are shown, which read, in an approximate translation:*
The earth covers one who was as Nestor in judgement;
The people mourn one who was a Socrates in wit;
Olympus possesses one who was a Virgil in art.

favourite, to Dr. John Hall, a physician of good reputation in that country. She left one child only, a daughter, who was married first to Thomas Nash, Esq; and afterwards to Sir John Bernard of Abbington, but died likewise without issue.

This is what I could learn of any note, either relating to himself or family. The character of the man is best seen in his writings; but since Ben Jonson has made a sort of an essay towards it in his *Discoveries*, though as I have before hinted, he was not very cordial in his friendship, I will venture to give it in his words:

> I remember the players have often mentioned it as an honour to Shakespeare, that in writing (whatsoever he penned) he never blotted out a line. My answer hath been, *Would he had blotted a thousand*, which they thought a malevolent speech. I had not told posterity this, but for their ignorance, who chose that circumstance to commend their friend by, wherein he most faulted. And to justify mine own candour, (for I loved the man, and do honour his memory, on this side idolatry, as much as any). He was indeed, honest, and of an open and free nature, had an excellent fancy, brave notions, and gentle expressions; wherein he flowed

> with that facility, that sometimes it was necessary he should be stopped: *Sufflaminandus erat*, as Augustus said of Haterius. His wit was in his own power, would rule of it had been so too. Many times he fell into those things could not escape laughter; as when he said in the person of Cæsar, one speaking to him, 'Cæsar thou dost me wrong.' He replied: 'Cæsar did never wrong, but with just cause' and such like, which were ridiculous. But he redeemed his vices with his virtues: there was ever more in him to be praised than to be pardoned.

As for the passage which he mentions out of Shakespeare, there is somewhat like it in *Julius Cæsar*, but without the absurdity; nor did I ever meet with it in any edition that I have seen, as quoted by Mr. Jonson. Besides his plays in this edition, there are two or three ascribed to him by Mr. Langbain, which I have never seen, and know nothing of. He writ likewise, *Venus and Adonis*, and *Tarquin and Lucrece*, in stanzas, which have been printed in a late collection of poems. As to the character given of him by Ben Jonson, there is a good deal true in it; but I believe it may be as well expressed by what Horace says of the first Romans, who wrote tragedy upon the Greek models, (or indeed translated them) in his *Epistle to Augustus*:

Natura sublimis et acer
Nam spirat tragicum satis et fæliciter audet,
Sed turpem putat in chartis metuitque lituram.*

There is a book of poems, published in 1640, under the name of Mr. William Shakespeare, but as I have but very lately seen it, without an opportunity of making any judgment upon it, I won't pretend to determine, whether it be his or no.

* *Epistles*, II, i, 165. 'Being gifted in spirit and vigour, for he has some tragic inspiration, and is happy in his ventures, but in ignorance, deeming it disgraceful, hesitates to blot.' – (trans. Loeb)

ILLUSTRATION CREDITS

Illustrations to Shakespeare's plays are all taken from Nicholas Rowe's edition of the works of Shakespeare, published in 1709. See Note on the Illustrations, p. 29 for further details

Cover and p. 18: The 'Chandos' portrait of Shakespeare, possibly by Joseph Taylor, c. 1610. National Portrait Gallery. Cover photograph Alamy

Endpapers and pp 40–41: Wenceslas Hollar, Long View of London from Bankside, 1647, using sketches made c. 1638

Half title: Shakespeare's Head, printer's emblem used by Jacob Tonson (this example from a book printed in 1735)

Frontispiece: Portrait of Shakespeare from the title page of the First Folio, engraved by Martin Droeshout, 1623

Opposite table of contents: View of the Globe theatre, detail from the panorama of London engraved by Claes Jansz. Visscher, in 1616 but possibly using earlier sketches

p 8: Nicholas Rowe, engraving by Michael Vandergucht after Sir Godfrey Kneller, Bt, published 1715

p 15: Thomas Betterton, engraving by Michael Vandergucht after Sir Godfrey Kneller, Bt, published 1710

p 21: Joseph Nash, William Shakespeare brought before the magistrate at Charlecote Park, colour lithograph, 1841

p 27: George Vertue, Antiquary admiring the memorial bust of William Shakespeare in Holy Trinity Church, Stratford upon Avon, October 1737. From Vertue's manuscript notebook A.y, BM Add. MS. 23092, fol. 17

p. 28: General frontispiece to Rowe's edition; see p. 29

p. 32: Portrait of Shakespeare by Benoît Arlaud, engraved Gaspard Duchange, 1709; see pp. 29–30

p. 33: Heading and tailpiece of Rowe's Life of Shakespeare from its original edition, 1709

p. 38: Henry Peacham (?), Sketch of a performance of Titus Andronicus, *c.* 1595 (?), Longleat

p 43: Johannes de Witt, redrawn by Aernout van Buchell, Sketch of the interior of the Swan Theatre in 1596. From Buchel's MS *Adversaria*, University Library, Utrecht